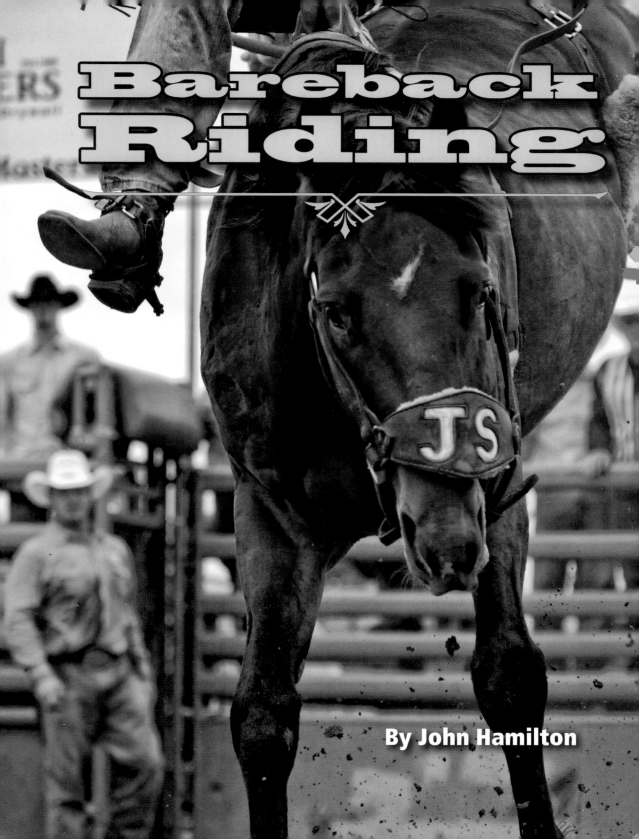

Bareback Riding

By John Hamilton

Visit us at
www.abdopublishing.com

Published by ABDO Publishing Company, PO Box 398166, Minneapolis, MN 55439. Copyright ©2014 by Abdo Consulting Group, Inc. International copyrights reserved in all countries. No part of this book may be reproduced in any form without written permission from the publisher. A&D Xtreme™ is a trademark and logo of ABDO Publishing Company.

Printed in the United States of America, North Mankato, Minnesota.
052013
092013

Editor: Sue Hamilton
Graphic Design: John Hamilton
Cover: John Hamilton
Photos: All photos by John Hamilton, except: Corbis-pg 6; Tom Baker-pg 10.

ABDO Booklinks
Web sites about rodeos are featured on our Book Links pages. These links are routinely monitored and updated to provide the most current information available. Web site: www.abdopublishing.com

Library of Congress Control Number: 2013931675

Cataloging-in-Publication Data

Hamilton, John.
 Bareback riding / John Hamilton.
   p. cm. -- (Xtreme rodeo)
 ISBN 978-1-61783-977-1
 1. Bronc riding--Juvenile literature. I. Title.
 791.8/4--dc23

                    2013931675

Contents

Bareback Riding

Some cowboys compare bareback riding to riding a jackhammer with one hand. With no saddle and only a single handhold to steady themselves, cowboys must use their strength, timing, and agility to ride a jumping, twisting horse and look graceful doing it.

History

It wasn't until the 1912 Calgary Stampede in Canada that bareback riding became an official rodeo event. Bareback riders point out that when people first learned to tame horses, they had to ride without saddles. So, even though bareback riding is a "new" rodeo event, it has been around for as long as people have been riding horses.

Jim Shoulders (left) was one of the greatest all-around rodeo stars that ever lived. He was called the Babe Ruth of rodeo cowboys. Shoulders won four bareback riding world championships in the 1950s. He was inducted into the Pro Rodeo Hall of Fame in Colorado Springs, Colorado, in 1979.

Rules

Bareback rides start in a small pen called a bucking chute. When the cowboy is ready, he raises his free hand, nods his head, and the gate is opened. A full ride lasts for eight seconds. The cowboy must hang on to the horse using only one hand. His free hand must be kept in the air. If it touches the horse or his own body or equipment, the judges give him a no-score.

Rigging

Bareback riders must stay on a wild, twisting bronc using only one hand. There is no saddle, or stirrups. To stay on the horse, the cowboy grips a suitcase-like handle attached to a rawhide strap. This device is called a rigging. It is strapped around the horse atop its withers (between the shoulder blades).

The handle of the rigging has just enough room for a cowboy to grip it with his gloved hand. Sticky resin is often used to help him grip the handle more firmly.

Rigging

11

Marking Out

Before the bronc makes its first jump out of the bucking chute, the rider must have both spurs touching above the horse's shoulders. This is called "marking out." The rider must keep the spurs in this position until after the horse's front feet hit the ground. This gives the horse an advantage. If the cowboy fails to mark out, he is disqualified.

Spurring Action

To receive a high score, the bareback rider demonstrates he's in control during even the wildest ride. When the horse bucks, the rider pulls his knees up and rolls his spurs along the horse's shoulders. When the horse comes down, he tries to straighten his legs, toes pointed out, above the horse's shoulders. A good ride is like a fluid dance, with the cowboy reacting and adjusting to every bone-jarring buck and twist.

Bucking spurs are blunt and turn freely. Horses and bulls have very thick hides, and are not hurt by rodeo spurs.

scoring

There are two kinds of professional rodeo competitions: timed events and rough stock events. In timed events, like barrel racing, riders compete against the clock and each other. In rough stock events, like bareback or saddle bronc riding, scores are based on the performance of the rider and the animal.

Two judges each give the cowboy a score ranging from 1 to 25 points. Cowboys who have smooth rides with good spurring action get higher scores. Grace and rhythm are important. The bronc is also scored from 1 to 25 points. High-scoring broncs give powerful rides, with lots of high-kicking action and changes of direction. The judges add their scores, for a total possible of 100 points. A score in the high 80s is considered a very good ride.

Equipment

Bareback riders supply their own rigging, which can cost several hundred dollars. They also need bucking spurs with rounded rowels (the metal tips). Clothing includes jeans, chaps, cowboy boots, long-sleeved shirt, and a Western-style hat. Special padded vests are often worn that protect the ribs in case the rider falls. A neck brace is also sometimes worn to prevent whiplash.

Special gloves made of steerhide or deerskin are used to grip the rigging handle.

Pickup Men

The pickup man is the rodeo cowboy's best friend. When the eight-second ride is over, sometimes the bronc keeps bucking, or gallops away from the exit.

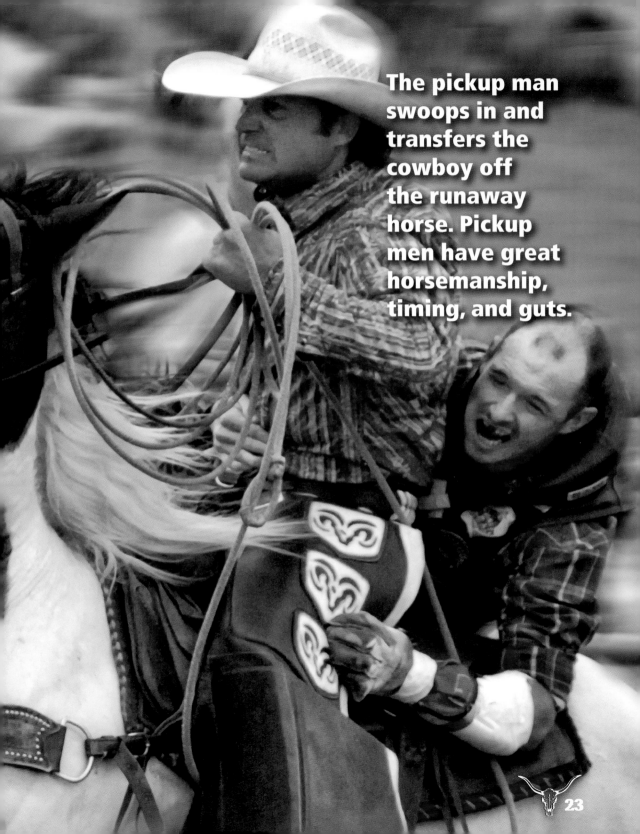

The pickup man swoops in and transfers the cowboy off the runaway horse. Pickup men have great horsemanship, timing, and guts.

23

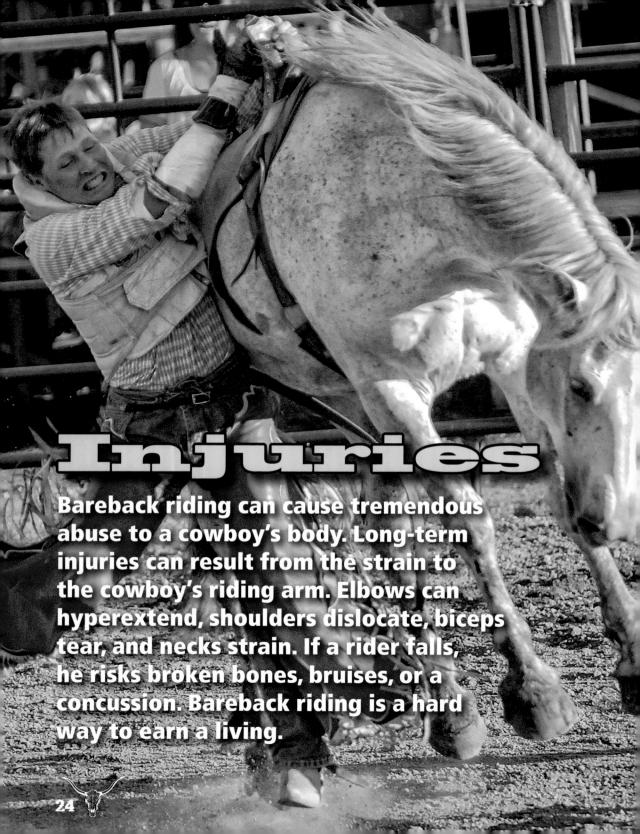

Injuries

Bareback riding can cause tremendous abuse to a cowboy's body. Long-term injuries can result from the strain to the cowboy's riding arm. Elbows can hyperextend, shoulders dislocate, biceps tear, and necks strain. If a rider falls, he risks broken bones, bruises, or a concussion. Bareback riding is a hard way to earn a living.

Horses

Bareback riding horses are usually smaller than saddle broncs. They are also faster and more agile. They are bred to buck. The best horses kick high and twist in many directions. Riders prize the most high-spirited horses. The more thrilling the ride, the higher the potential score.

A horse that bucks
with a lot of
power is called an
"arm jerker."

RAM

27

Animal Care

Rodeo livestock are an expensive investment. The Professional Rodeo Cowboys Association (PRCA) has strict rules to make sure rodeo livestock are treated humanely. The vast majority of animals are very well cared for. A flank strap is a fleece-lined strap snugged under the horse's belly. It is tightened as the horse leaves the bucking chute. It encourages the horse to extend its hind legs.

Some people think the flank strap is too tight and causes pain for the horse. However, this is not true. The strap does not cause pain. In fact, if it is drawn too tight, the horse will stop bucking.

Glossary

Calgary Stampede

Held annually in Calgary, Alberta, Canada, the Calgary Stampede is a rodeo that traces its roots to the late 1800s. More than one million people attend each year.

Chaps

Leather or suede leg coverings. They are buckled on over trousers. Working cowboys use chaps while riding on horseback through heavy brush. Rodeo chaps are colorful and have a lot of fringe. The flapping fringe makes a ride seem even more exciting.

Flank Strap

A fleece-covered leather strap that is secured with a buckle and snugged under a horse or bull's belly near the sensitive flank area. It encourages them to extend their rear legs, but does not cause pain.

Free Hand

Bareback, saddle bronc, and bull riders can hang on with only one hand. Their free hand must not touch the animal or themselves, or they are disqualified.

Mark Out

During the bareback or saddle bronc's first jump out of the chute, the cowboy's spurs must touch the top of the animal's shoulders.

Rough Stock

Untamed horses and bulls.

Index